Dedications

I0078116

To:

my Muppetus - my hope

Mi Preciosa - my joy

-and-

my Squirrel - my heart

To my mother: I'm sorry I'm so late. You should've gotten the first copy. Hopefully we'll get to talk about it someday.

And to Nyddia H.: you kick started this back in senior year and I promised I'd dedicate this to you, so here you go.

Scribblevisions

i'll run out of words
before i run out of thoughts
to put those words to...

Bear - 04/11/14

Foreword

If you've never been to a poetry show, then you've been missing out on a beautiful art form. If you've never stayed after a poetry show and talked to those who performed, then you've been missing out on a captivating community. They say abs are made in the kitchen, and I say performers are made during communion. I met Bear at exactly this kind of supper table. We each poured out ink blood on stage and we each were nourished on the bread of criticism. We each seemed to appreciate the other's recipe and we kept coming back for seconds.

Bear's work demands that you refill your plate time and time again. Keep a dictionary close at hand. See 3/26/17 for example. I am thankful to know a poet who keeps the standard of the art high. He and I have discussed the essence of poetry, what sets it apart, how performing it changes it, and how to stay true to the art while trying to convey what's on our hearts. I read Bear's work and converse with him because I can't afford an MFA program.

"of winter," one of the few titled poems, reminds me of the kinds of poems we read in English class. This is one of those poems that makes non-poets laugh, because snow can't really be mesmerizing enough to inspire verse. Except for when it is.

Bear uses all of the sophisticated literary devices: internal rhyme, hidden rhyme, and alliteration. He also seems to have effortless rhyme and flow that come only from mastery of sonic language. He's like a rapper without anything shackling him to a beat or a form.

Through reading this book, I can feel the hues of emotion in the search for a forever smile, a forever love. "Mornings" is the perfect blend of poetry and the jazz music that has always held a tender spot in my heart. Like, "of winter," it takes a common and simple concept and makes it utterly brilliant. It takes nothing for granted but magnifies it all, putting each facet on display.

Bear posits why the "caged bird screams" and the stars tell him stories. He has dreams, and obviously poems, in his pockets. This book compelled me to believe in his ability to "carry forever" and believe *again* in "a love that knows me."

Happy reading.

June '18
Najah Amatullah Hylton

Scribblevisions

Thoughts and Theories from the Third Lane

words twist into the delicate blades of an airborne melody, a rhapsody in blue hues fused across souls that have just met...i forget where i was going when i met you, but found my destination inscribed across your smile...whiling away hours upon eternities in reflection, perfecting each nuance as our hands met across promise and passion, fashioning a forevermore out of just one more today...we play at sorrow and confusion, building blocks of boldness that ballast our trip through this life together...it's all a game, these questions and unknowns, because we are built together and forever, and winning is as natural as the breaths i take for and with you...it is true that i've known love before, but this time it seems to know me, and really, that makes all the difference...

04/16/14 - 2

my life is painted across the ever-expanding tapestry of the heavens with a coarse brush of fine-edged destiny...electric hues of grays and blues paint over the used and frayed fringes of a torn and tattered soul...bold, broad sweeps of silence and tight-printed plaintive points of fear bespeckle that canvas in prismatic sanctimony...clashing crayola sketches of flight and fancy mix with the watered-down pastels of patience gone awry...my soul is tattooed on the sky...

forevers

i loved you a forever ago, a forever that was shorter than my definition of eternity...silly me to think our hearts ticked to the same clock, 'cause when you blocked me from your rhythm, the schism i felt between our souls disrupted my mechanisms...isn't it funny how short a forever turns out to be...you promised a you and me, but the you i see has left this me alone to his devices...the memory of your proximity is all that suffices in this loneliness and were it only so simple to live in those bygone yesterdays without these tattered today's infiltrating my smile...i bought a new jacket today because my arm was so cold; it's the one on the side you promised to always be by...i found some new thread to sew that patch that read "us" and was supposed to plug that hole in my heart you started to mend but ran out of time or desire to wire completely shut...what happened to that forever...were i a touch more clever i'd sever my dreams from this foolishly labeled hope, deal myself enough rope to swing to my freedom and see what other's forevers have to offer...but i'm just not that smart...so, stupidly i cling to those beliefs that bring me a grief i couldn't describe had i an entire forever to try...or maybe i'll just use that forever you cast aside; i think it's still got some room left...

...she don't love me no more, that is, if she ever did...she ran and hid her heart in a shoebox stuffed in the back of the closet labeled "mine: don't touch"...was it too much to ask for just a little peek? probably so, 'cause my own heart was stuck on the top shelf behind too many someone else's that crisscrossed it like bars of pain in a prison of wishing and wanting...i don't know if i love her no more, that is, if i ever really knew i did...we bid for a romance, raised the stakes in this eternal game, tied our names together in the priciest twine and said those "i'll forever be thine's" in a perfect memory captured in the photograph she took...i can't even look for it 'cause she stuck it in that shoebox, this time in a brand new closet, in a brand new place, in a brand new tomorrow to which i aint being invited...

of winter

...in the midst of it, trees stretch barren fingers to this fragile sky, bleak and broken by shards of birdsong, muffled in the white...grasping fingers scrape and mutter under a dance of wind, bending and seeking the furry hermits in their homes, tucked so expertly against the chill...silent, solemn, endless sheets of tranquility beneath which the battle of green is already waging...yellows and golds and reds and the effortless, dauntless, ravenous green waits just beneath, urging and surging toward the sign of the new sun...but not today...no, today is silence and solemnity and serenity under endless sheets of crystallized sky...

...to the girl with the smile that changed my life...my apologies for letting that smile get away...i thought i'd learned all the words i'd needed to say to keep that face with those lips that smiled that smile in my life forever, but forever was a drop in a bucket i proved not to be man enough to carry...nary a day passes that that smile doesn't haunt my daydreams and it seemed it had been lost to me forever, but clever boy i am i searched and i swam the seas of memories and docked at the harbor of happenstance that brought my heart back to that smile...and the years i'd filed away as lost and incomplete suddenly found relief in the unwavering sunshine of that smile -- which now held two smaller smiles that themselves looked like your smile colored with the tints of another...now you're a mother, a wife, a life made whole on a whole 'nother shore and once more i felt myself being cast adrift by missed opportunity...i feign immunity to the imperishable pressure of regret but that's just because i set my soul on an endless tether and let it wander from the moorings of my face, but were i willing to trace the lines back to my heart i'd be forced to admit that a part of me died when your smile cried out "liar!" from behind a frozen screen...i'd promised you rings and forget-me-not's, the one tarnished, the other slightly withered, but gathered in faithfulness nonetheless and at your request i held them until you deemed us ready...but the course is ordained, if not necessarily steady, and our ships were bound for disparate lands...so though my hand remained half raised in a hailing gesture of eternal sustain, your same shaded eyes to a home i could not conquer...so while i've wandered in shadow and shade, stricken by grins and facetious smirks, your smile lurked in the corners of a globe i've only come to realize is much smaller than even 'they' could profess...so now you bless another heart with the brightest rays of happiness i've ever known man to hope to muster, and i bluster my way through another day of smile-denied memory and regret...so forget you, that smile...i curse you, that smile...i hate you, that smile -- and i love how just saying "that smile" makes me feel...

ode to the girl with the smile that changed my life...

Mornings

mornings are jazz songs written on the tablature of the street by feet
moving in hustling syncopation...heels clicking riffs against concrete
snares, bass lines that take time to build as toes tickle the backbeat
of street scenes in complex inner ear harmony, "pardon me's"
melodic interludes infused with ivory and ebon promises,
effortlessly gliding and soaring through notes the people ain't
invented yet...the cityscape is one vast page of players just getting
tuned up...sun crescendos over a slow build horizon, wizened old
spirits start playing prayers in toothless smiles that still have
bite...the last dregs of night are drunk in the full cups of horns
formed by hands, mouths and ears all geared toward another day
among this careful human cacophony...against the backdrop of a
paper moon I hear Birds reeling Dizzily over Miles of blank canvas,
Tranes screaming along slick hip tracks, while Monks cling to the
rails like prayers made before pearls in a twirling, lilting drift of an
endless rubato...chests heave with ostinato life, pouring sight into
the sonically blinded, high minded connoisseurs of fire and fury,
luring the unhurried deeper into the soundscape...stakes are pulled
and released during an aural feast of "hello's" and "thank you's" and
the take two's of the rush through late doors, black gold pouring
over harmonies and hearts, starting the sweet, deep kick of another
integral part to the song...

02/03/15

i looked in a mirror into the eyes of your reflection and smiled because you were looking at me...but refraction aint as exact a science as they portray, for the eyes you were watching walked away and i was left to stay and smile at somebody else's memory...

02/03/15 - 2

my heart goes where my head cannot follow...my head leads where my heart cannot stomach...my stomach quails at the places my feet have landed...my feet keep dancing back to you...

02/13/15

i stuff my feelings in the pockets of my poetry, stuff them down deep with the lint and the crumbs and the lost paperclips and ink pens...tuck them away from prying hearts and reaching eyes...i crumple them into tight little balls of forgetfulness and ambivalence, scribble my sanity along curved lines of blue and red, lines of sorrow and anger, tears and frustration, silence and passion...they line my pockets like otherwordly currency, passports to nowhere and everywhere, part of all and nothing...my feelings, tokens deferred, dreams unsought...there, in the forgotten depths of my pockets...

i stopped answering the calls for pick-me-ups because you never pick up when i call you...and you never stop to pick me up when i call on you...this relationship is a pickup game where everyone's dropped the ball...one call, one reaction, one interaction, no satisfaction, just endless tripping wires crossing our intentions...one for today, one for tomorrow, you sow my sorrow with your cast off frivolities, my feelings reeling in the backdraft of your burning indifference...and i get it...yeah, i see it and i understand..."that man," not this, until you miss his last kiss and your tears float you down the river back to me...but i'm not gonna be here, see, cause i've pulled my cord out of the wall...all i ask is a two way connection, some acknowledgment of affection, some direction to take this thing in that's at least partially positive...but that line still aint jingling...i don't mean to single you out; you're one of many, just like the rest, and though you promised to be best and at my behest swore to stay, you wandered back into your familiar realm of my-heart-be-damned...okay...i'm okay...as long as the next time your hand strays to the dial you file it under "wish i could have" 'cause i will have blocked your number on the inbound service of my life...and don't even think of calling me collect...

we're all chasing down dreams but are too scared to sleep...waking moments become faint memories of hopes realized in slumber, and numbered days count forward into iniquity far more often than eternity...voices crying in the darkness, alone except for echoes, and we are absolutely sure that nobody knows, even though ours is a chorus of the lost and alone and lonely...voices crying out in the darkness, a harmony of hard hearts and harder hearths, cold and still, filled with the dreams of yesternight...i'd cry were it not so hard, broken tears, shards of leftover dreams...dreams...if they come...

sometimes life hits you so hard that it leaves a mark...in time the bruises on your soul will fade, the broken bones of your hopes will knit, but there will be a scar...there will always be the scar...

i wish i could call you and you'd answer…i wish i knew you were there by the phone, waiting for me to call, wanting for me to call as much as i want to call out to you…i wish my heart knew it was safe to dial, safe to pluck out those numbers i've never forgotten, simple digits that play so many tricks with my mind…i don't mind if you're somewhere else with someone else…i don't mind if your time doesn't include the turns of my clock…i just want a piece of the pieces you call a life…just a sliver of the dream i woke up for specifically…i just wish i had the comfort of a call, a word, a thought, a concern, a care…i wish i had the confidence to call…

05/25/15

tried to find the threads to sew our relationship back together, but you kept handing me scissors...don't know it these memories will ever find you...i didn't wish to bind you to my hopes, but i hoped at least you'd want to be a part of the party...seems i couldn't conquer the Apple a day, so i'll play it out to oranges...i'll go and forage for another friendship now, and pray it won't sail quite so readily beyond my reach...into the breach, dear heart, into the breach, and should some day you beseech my love, may it still be willing to wander...we shall see...

she was a "round the way" girl: round hips swirling with every step and tilt curved like her lips in a disdainful smile as her stride ate up the miles between her right now and my "hey, miss; how you be?"…she had x-ray vision so could see through the lies and bullsh*t but she hesitated to put them on, instead singing songs of someday that in some way mollified her malfeasance with just the right hint of mischief clearly designed to drive us wild…filed under "out of our league" she was a teasing temptress, the simplest form of a myriad muses, fused with light and life yet teetering on the knife-like edge of shadows…who knows what she thinks as she blinks away tears she should never have to shed…who knows how unwelcoming the ever-invited bed…who knows how often she's been led down the path of her own destruction while instructing the path to salvation…maybe it will just take patience to teach her something better, a jumbled jangle of letters scripted across her possibles in cascading waves of self-affirmations…or maybe it's just a late night call, a post on her wall, a ten letter text in which less is invariably more…who knows…she's that girl from around the way, and as her hips dip and sway beyond our sight i can't help thinking that she'd stop if i just found the right way to say "hi"…

sometimes you sit there in the night and wonder just where your heart is going...where will it lead, what is its destination, what its hopes and fortunes and future...sometimes you sit there alone in the darkness and wonder if anyone hears you in that silence, in that murky mystery...sometimes you wonder if you ever truly heard yourself...and sometimes the night follows you into the day, a shadow of the soul that bleeds its fingers of searching solitude into the waking habits, collapsing and coalescing around the best of your intentions...and then you find yourself in that darkness again, alone in that darkness, all alone in the night...

08/23/15

I know why the caged bird screams...wings pressed against the bars of a universe too small, talons clutching a thousand eternities, fire and light and rage railing against a weak and timorous reality...yes, I know why the caged bird screams -- and why only the silence screams back...

i wanna be

i wanna be your morning memory after a nighttime revelry, the smell on your skin when you blend your coffee with the perfect kiss of cream…i wanna hear you scream on the inside of your dreams and burst the seams of your aspirations, exhalations of lust on the bust of an archaic composer, breaking your composure while exposing your laughter to unprepared passersby…i wanna spread you across the sky and dive into the infinity, scribbling eternity across our wishes like dishes best served cold and bold and brash and unrepentant…i want to be an instant that's forever, a slow motion dance together as light but piercing as a feather into all your smiling places…put me through my paces as we run this life together, straight to the top without stopping or thinking or questioning or blinking, just streaming like ionized matter across a perfect 'spanse of heaven…just you and i and heaven…forever…you and i and heaven…

you forgot me...another smile came a'calling and you put me on the shelf to wait...there among your dusty memories, among those sad, lost yesterday's I sat to wait and wonder...there, next to the box of tears and fears you once entrusted to my keeping, the key my promise to never let you go...back by the picture of the smile that was supposed to live next to my name, now torn and faded by someone else's today...back on the shelf of your life, back in your box of maybes and might be's and some days..back until his smile fades, until yours dims, until your heart needs it's memories...back where you have forgotten me...

03/26/16

a million unanswered questions, each one numbered in a notebook stuffed at the back of my heart...at the start it was all so simple, so earnest, so perfect, this life plan made manifest with just the barest hint of effort...but time and grief and longing wore away the edges of awareness, of surety, of certainty and left those million unanswered questions...they say that there are lessons in losing, and maybe I'm just confusing hope with horror, but I've borrowed my fair share of waiting and the well has run to dust...just one from those million would be sufficient...just one among those million questions...just one to find the answer...

I don't wanna do bad things but i'm trapped in bad choices, trying to fend off the voices of tongues that speak trouble...the handsome little bubble I'd built around myself popped and now I can't stop the intrusion of confusion that's a malady to my melody...I don't know if I can sing my way out of this one, but I sho' ain't weak enough to cry...all these bad choices...just one phone call away...

...hands on the thread of night, fingers on the pulse of the sky, listening to the narrative of the stars as they tell stories beyond our memories...there's life beyond our vision, wisdom beyond our hearing, truth that exists beyond the words available to speak it, just an endless expanse of knowing, littered like leaves against all the realm of probability...there is much of life there beyond our ability to know...

...there is the ever and interminable weight that sits upon and betwixt us, formed of our need to be righteous, forged of our propensity to do wrong...

I feel like I'm cheating on you with my hopes and dreams, like my mistress is wishing and wanting and hope...I love you, but it seems so incomplete, so timid and frail because I rail against all the things that you aren't...

01/11/17

i do not give my poems names; i give them dates...i do this because i do not think names are very important...names just clutter up ideas...instead i give my poems dates because they are the chronicle of my place in this time...

03/07/17

with what hope were we as seeds planted into this time…with such promise the promise of life was given…how full the purpose that was set to course through our veins, a river of will unleashed in rivulets of succor…how great the hope, those pillars upon which our futures are cemented...

You Are

He looked at her and smiled.

"You are something else," he said.

"What am I?" she asked, face tweaked into a mocking grin.

He took her hips in his hands and slid close as her breath quickened.

"Thick like new molasses but twice as strong. Sweet as winter milk, warm and heavy. Solid like forever, wisdom pouring from your pores like the dreams of eternity. And aloof, like a goddess sitting astride the bulking back of night, sight cast into the hearts and minds of men long given to loss and lust at your feet. You are perfection made mortal, sight made to touch, a kiss of sunlight and midnight sharing space and time."

"All that?" she asked, her hands circling his back and drawing him closer.

"All that," he breathed into the nape of her neck. "And mine."

in rills and rivulets, love finds its way wending through our little patch of forevers...clever words and secret smiles are filed away in banks of eternity, learning me and you and us as we go...slow and so persistent, insisting on something much greater and deeper, keeping in tune with the harmonics that make heaven stop and shudder...wonder and light and love and liking just being with and next to you...these are my words and intentions...and you...you, my love, are my song...

03/19/17 – 2

tell me what care looks like...how does one write love? are there enough pages to stage the epic that epitomizes concern? do we learn from yearning anything other than new ways to hurt? is pain our only passion, penance the preacher to which we kneel in obeisance? are lessons just leading us to loss? tell me what care looks like -- so i'll know how to show it...

we are but hollow voices in a high wind, yelling in vain against the tide...inside we are researching the refrains of relevance, settling for impertinence and importunity, immune to the paucities of pride save that which we strip from good taste...racing to the edge of a loud and signifying nothingness, tumbling into inanity, too base for infamy, just petty baubles of light and sound caught on the foam...alone in the far-flung darkness, too pale to go beyond the pale, lost lights making mockery of our betters the stars...just hollow voices screaming against the gale, railing against fate and familiarity, parity and personality...just voices in the wind...

i'm full of words that wanna come out, wanna come out and see the sun, see the sun and play for awhile, play or just lay in the shade of a tree on a hill and feel one and part of the world…i'm full of words that wanna watch the clouds race across the sky, wanna skip rocks on a lake and watch ducks fly by, wanna sit on the knee of my father and ask why, words that just want their chance to live…i wanna give my words the assurance that they matter, give them comfort through the hard times ahead, prepare them for a road that's broken and bruised because it's had to fight past the constriction of my lungs…my words will have to fight their way from the bottom of my tears, swamped and deluged and tossed in the torrent of pains i won't even speak of with myself…my words will have to soothe the rage that tears at my spirit every time i hear another "no," another "go," another woe added to the mural on a wall too damned stubborn to fall…and my words will have to be the rage that inspires them to build cages to trap the fire that threatens the town that resented the beast and would see him leashed, but no longer…my words are hunger and savagery and soothsaying and songs playing and kids laying beneath a sky too blue to lie and why's and where's and there's and here's and near to all and everything because they are all and everything and everything is them, and me, and it, and us…i'm full of so many words that wanna come out…but mama said they gotta stay in today…

let me write words that spiral around your frame scribing your name in a torrent of soft touches and a cascade of kisses in near-misses of life meet lust and just a few more seconds before the explosion of both...let me write your seduction in sixty syllables that sink into your synapses like thirst made man and hunger made wo-man and the satiation of our ingratiation made perfect in rhythmic harmony...let me see you smile, just for me, just for we, just because we exist and existence begins where convention and normal share a backseat...i repeat: let me write the words you haven't yet heard, tell the stories you haven't yet possessed, the tales of time and life and love and living you've only now thought to wonder about...let me write these words on the tablet of your heart and the table of your flesh...and if you're brave enough, let me write them with my lips.......

We are, all of us, I think, existing in those spaces between broken moments, in those remnants of reflections, in the wishes that span the gulf of tarnished dreams and heartbreak.

We are, all of us, I think, walking a communal road of solitude, pieces of our wholes left littered in each other's wakes.

Mistakes are, at times, the only given, hidden between hope and hopelessness, outlining the lines by which our intentions are ordered.

We are all of us, I think, looking and learning, yearning and dreaming, hoping for a harmony as yet unplayed.

We are, all of us, I do believe...

Sparrow

It's not your fault, little bird, that you never learned to fly.

You were stuck in that cage they built for you,

Wings clipped by dreams deferred,

Words of power turned to words of pain,

And you sit in the rain of their indifference, cage shackled and hope bound against time.

It's not your fault, little bird, that you couldn't appreciate your plumage.

They told you proper birds were far less friendly,

Pretty birds were of necessity the same.

They tamed your song and made you parrot their disdain for yourself and other birds built to fly.

It's not your fault, little bird, that you can't help but ask why.

How many lies are you expected to eat as treats from the hand of a hateful master?

Disaster and calamity are the currency of vanity, shoved into your spirit, a violation of heaven.

That you should cry until seven times seventy becomes the rage of seven eternities would be no wonder, for you are wonderful and magnificent and glorious in your light.

You are flight, little bird, your wings made to capture, caress, cajole and control the wind.

You are light, little bird, your song a sound that serenades the stars.

You are right, little bird, the truth and the justice and the rhythm of our heartbeats.

You are life, little bird, and you can fly for us all.

You are flight, little bird, and from you I have learned to soar.

She was a song and he was the rupture of the anvil.

She was a vision and he an ocular occlusion.

She was the pulse and he was a myocardial infarction.

From the start they were destined to be broken.

Token words of love he'd write to her in spite of the distance of his heart,

Like two ships torn apart by the winds of hurricanes he knew the blame was atmosphere and circumstance, and while she danced like wind and the rain and the unbridled sun, he felt no closer to her or better than a few guilty letters hastily written and delivered.

Her smile shivered for forcing its way past his illusions, the salt solution of her eyelids were not kid by the reality in his strain.

She felt the pain, felt it as sure as she felt her ability to surpass it, to amass it in perfect billowing swarms of dreams and laughter, to tie it to the rafters like sage and sunlight, to make of night their loving and dusk their dawn, she'd draw him on and on and on into eternity.

Because he'd learn of she.

Oh, yes, he would learn and while he might spurn her affection and squirm against his own he would yield against its foam like shore meet sea and that death so familiar and inevitable in its embrace.

She was grace and he could fathom no other option.

Love was their only respite and respite he would just have to receive.

I write sentences without periods and filled with ellipses because I am trying to write immortality...if my words don't end my words *won't* end; I shall exist forever in the space that is breath and thought and purpose...I write my life in these words, by these words, through these words, yet still, just and simply, to be heard...for I am not merely writing words; i am writing life...life built on an ellipsis...

07/06/17

i sit at a table witnessing fables delivered by beleaguered men desiring a vision...writing myths against mirrors, in the glass they darkly beheld, well wishes fall off fingertips as lips concoct new stories and fictions...i sit in the lap of lies comforted by her familiar embrace...we're all shamed for the doing, all remanded to the same...we too few speak truth, and that less oft to ourselves...we are all stuck at tables writing fables we pray that others will believe...

07/21/17

haiku

I find in God's grace
A peace I've yet to conquer
And therefrom springs hope.

There are words that live in the silence of our hopes and dreams, valleys and streams we cross on our journey into self-understanding.

So many words demanding our attention, honorable mentions of value to our lives, those plateaus for which we strive just piecemeal propositions of peace.

Through each we release our folly and our fortunes, orphans of the stars carving our existence into the ether.

And of this are our monuments made, by such are we saved, and in that final refrain are the words that live and laugh their light in our waiting silence.

08/13/17

Somewhere out to sea

Standing at dark harbors harboring feelings of failed chances, glances missed and words unspoken, love and life long since broken, tokens of dreams too tarnished for this game.

I stand at harbors bereft of cargo, manifests misplaced, spaces where names belong empty and overwritten, hidden behind empty pages.

08/15/17

Situationships

"We are all but ships in the night, passing beyond sound and sight, our beacons blinking in the darkness. And sometimes we meet, find in one another common cause and course to travel along together. But weather and time and tide and life are ever flowing, and knowing naught of the place held us by fate, we will likely drift away. For we are all but ships passing in the night on an ocean of our own loneliness."

I keep thinking that forever will be better because the present costs too much.

Today's got too many ways to make tomorrow that much worse.

I sing verses of sermons hoping to find hope but keep having dreams about rope and a short swing into serenity.

There's gotta be greater in infinity, right?

There's that eternal morning that's supposed to supplant the night.

Even fighters get fostered after the fight.

I just feel like there's better in forever.

But it's something in that transition,

Something about that first step that is invariably the last, something about moving too fast and missing your exit.

I'm scared of that transition.

But I'm more scared of the fact that I keep wishing it'll come soon.

I just don't know if I have any more room for aches in this heart, if I've played out my scene and life's recast my part, and if there's more wisdom in going than staying, I definitely ain't that smart; I'm just asking for answers.

Just praying for chances...

i walked into a safe space, safe because i was in that space, 'cause
i'm a gaht dang Bear, and nobody in their right mind challenges a
bear…

and i stood in that space and said: "hear me, ye foolish! hear me, ye
blind! hear me, ye apathetically and arrogantly deaf!

i am ANGRY!

i am angry, and today you shall hear my voice!

i am the voice of those crying in the wilderness, sent there, marched
there, trailed there in tears and torment, homes and hope carved
from the lashes on their backs as the pain seeds the central plains
with a tale of guilt that would fester and bloom for generations…

i am the voice of midnight mermaids cast while thrashing into the
deep, bleating forth in bubbles a ballad of ballast that blasts closed
ears with a resounding shout of freedom in that watery embrace…

i am the cry that came from concrete, blood seeped in the ripped
rivulets that rivet this country to its tarnished, contemptible past; i
am the last of that breed that lived on its knees, for i have found my
feet and they march toward the curtain call of justice…

i am justice! i am righteousness! i am the pain of the slain, the shame
of the vain, the rain that falls upon Kapiti plain over which my
ancestor stands like the big stork bird and with hue and cry and
hailing word calls forth thunder and damnation from the heavens
you've attempted to paint as your own…

i am home! i am the tie that binds the continents, the wonder and
the rage writ on the pages of pyramids in heiroglyphs that higher
lift your eyes and awareness toward God...

i am the downtrodden, yes, but every seed committed to the earth is
just one drop of fire away from birth, and i am born, i am bloom, i
blossom, i am life...

hear me, ye foolish! hear me, ye who deafen yourselves with spite
and lies! hear me, ye loud and lost! hear me, for i too sing America!"

10/18/17

I wrote a poem for you today.

I wrote it in heartbeats on the inside of my soul.

Perhaps tomorrow you will read it in my smile.

11/06/17

Can a blistered soul pray?

Can it accept that God doesn't mind callouses?

Can the Balm of Gilead double as aloe vera for a heart burned by its
own shame?

Can tears count as time served?

Does pain grant an early release for good behavior?

Does the Savior count our stripes or His?

What is the perfect prayer to pray?

What is a sinner allowed to say?

Does God yet beckon or are we too far astray?

Will my knees find their way to the throne today...

I wanna feel you close to me and I feel like you're supposed to be, like it ain't just an "I want to" but an "I need to," an "I have to," an "I was built to," a "for this purpose was I born to."

I wanna feel your skin speak to mine, each cell and sprinkle of melanin telling stories of their own while our lungs share songs as we breathe and our teeth tell tales as we smile and our ears say "I love you" as they embrace the taste of words we've outgrown the need to say.

I wanna stay with you forever, and literally forever, like past life and past heaven and past the past and beyond space, just you and me in a realm that defies the term "place," sitting by God's throne laughing about that time we were young and foolish enough to think we weren't gonna be together.

I don't even wanna be clever anymore.

I don't wanna try to make you smile or laugh or think of me or feel some kind of way in my presence.

Cause I wanna get past that.

I wanna outlast that.

I want that to be a given just as sure as we live living, as sure as this gift's given, as sure as He's been risen, I want it to be that concrete.

I wanna be complete and so I wanna be next to you.

I want to fit in your spaces like a puzzle, your arms to be the muzzle that clamp down on my fears, your fingertips the tools that deconstruct my tears, your love the infinite ruler by which we measure our years,

I wanna be complete in you.

And I wanna see me in you, our purpose and plans, dreams and aspirations as tightly twined as shared strands of DNA, genetically composed to be exactly this way, I wanna pray and you say amen, wanna say I love you and you reply "til when," want you as my first, my last, my then, I just wanna be with you.

And I kinda want you to feel the same about me.

A little bit.

Just a little bit.

Kinda sorta...

I think of you when I ought not.

I got caught not paying attention in a life lesson and had to ask the Professor's forgiveness,

"It's just this smile on my mind," I tell him. "I just can't forget it. She smiles and my lips dance in answer. She speaks and my ears tune like satellites. Her eyes make mine wish they could see right before my heart gets left. I step in her footsteps because I wanna walk in her shoes, absorb each scrape, scratch, heartache and bruise, stick so close to her skin that our follicles fuse. I'm just caught up, you see."

I'm afraid to say it, afraid to release those words to the ether, afraid to submit that prayer to the reverb, afraid if I lose myself I can't keep her, afraid of being afraid.

She makes me that way.

But then she takes that away.

Takes my fear and replaces it with peace, takes my emptiness and lays a feast, takes my storm of doubt and tells the winds to cease, she has the power to make me still.

So I submit my will.

Submit to her.

Submit and commit, we both one to the other, as standing before God and my holy big brother, I hand her the reins to my heart for I will follow no other from this day and until eternity shall come.

Someday...

If she'll just pick up the phone...

Tell me, shorty: what does your heart look like? Why you holding so tight to a dream and can't wake up?

Folk are meant to take up spaces in our daytime, fill the pockets of sunshine that pool around our yesterdays.

But they ain't for every tomorrow.

Who you tryna borrow your smile from?

And why?

Don't you already know how to smile?

You've been doing it for awhile, now.

Tell me how it got lost -- and who took it.

Look: folk are made to take up the daytime, but love was built specifically for the night.

It's that right feeling when everybody else has left, that sensation of peace after a whole slew of storms, that warm silence between people that don't need words.

I've heard it.

I could even say I hear it though I ain't nowhere near it and yet I still can say it exists.

So tell me miss, what does your heart look like?

And do you even remember...

Useful

I took a test today, an internet triviality that tried to break down
reality into an amusing anecdote.

It *quote* "wanted to see how you see yourself," and as I was
currently engaged with nothing else I shrugged and said, "Sure, I'll
play along."

So the gist of the mission was to determine what kind of person you
are by comparing you to a household object.

Who doesn't love objectification, amirite?

But I'd committed myself, and anyone who knows me knows that
once I commit, that's it.

So into the fray I marched, boldly and hopefully, my mouse the
mighty sword that would carve out my fate.

And it was going along pretty great.

The questions began:

One: "Are you more often the friend or the lover?"

Two: "Are you an only child but still everyone's brother?"

Three: "Are you the life of the party or did they misplace the
invite?"

Four: "Do you get your 'wyd' only in daylight?"

Five: "Is your phone filled with pages of other people's problems?"

And, finally:

"If you were suddenly not around would they care that you weren't
there to solve them?"

Now, I'm no expert, but these seemed like some pretty serious and pointed questions, a lot more so than I expected.

While I digested just what this all portended, I clicked the button marking the exercise complete, curious, and, were I being honest, somewhat concerned as to what it would reveal.

The test finished its figuring, amalgamated its algorithm and parsed out its result:

As it turns out, I am a paper clip.

A paper clip.

Of all things to be, a paper clip.

At this exact moment I am both a paper clip and very, very confused.

Obligingly, the test proffered its reasoning.

According to some wise and mysterious foreign teenager with access to wifi and HTML, I am "useful but not necessary. Everyone needs you -- when they need you. They'll hunt you down with fire and fervor when things are falling apart. You keep the fluttering and funny pieces of their life together -- for a time. And then one day you'll simply vanish. You'll go into a crowded drawer of social media memories, or under a stack of texts they couldn't once wait to send, or into a pocket that used to hold a hand that used to hold yours but now only holds friendship and lint and promises and pencil tips way down in its crusty and crowded crevices. You're useful; everyone needs you, everyone wants you, everyone has to have you -- and every last one will forget you were ever there."

I stared at the screen for long moments, stared at the words that dared to print in virtual ink a proclamation of some tyrant and disdainful god, stared at the temerity with which this test deigned itself capable of describing my life, stared and stared at the msg I sent two days ago that you just forgot to read and return because you've been busy, you've been working, you've been trying but life's been hectic and I should respect it because, hey, I matter. I'm important. Maybe not so shiny anymore. Maybe a little dented. Maybe I've already held all the pieces of your life I was factory-made to fit. Maybe that's it.

But I still matter.

I'm still important.

I'm still useful.

I'm still

useful...

There's this spacious silence behind my eyelids where your name echoes like a lullaby.

The melody is one I can't quite remember, can't quite recall, but it's so entwined in my being that I know it instinctively.

It whispers past my past, touching and playing over the man I used to be, images and pictures of hopes and dreams unfinished and unfurnished, burnished by the kindly light of time.

It dances over my todays, keeping me honest, however painful, disdainful of my illusions, scoffing at delusions of grandeur, requiring only truth in my purpose and mission.

And it sings into my tomorrow, it's voice leading the way to places not yet seen but imagined, crystallized in hope, wrapped in aspiration, steeped in salvation, a thousand tomorrows and each one greater than the thousand before.

There's this echoing space behind my eyelids filled with the silence of sound, round and enveloping, fulsome and everlasting, enraptured by the playing of your name...

i remember being a kid and being sooo excited to go to the library...

i remember it being like an adventure, a vacation taken weekly,

around and down the corner to that sacred and magical place...

i remember the day i got my first library card, my name inked with

permanence and diligence and responsibility; i was allowed to

check out books! i was allowed to master knowledge!

i remember the smells, the sensation of the carpet under my

sneakers, the sound of thoughts tumbling through the ozone and

ether of that self-contained universe...

visions and ideas and idle ideals swirled in cascading rhythms,

dancing against the backs of eyes on which were playing a

thousand different scenes of life trapped in language...

i remember finding my favorite aisle, filled with books crafted just

to fit my hands...

i remember distant lands and their inhabitants, dragons and lions

and witches and wardrobes and child detectives and tiny people

with furry feet, and light and laughter and adventure on repeat

again and again and again...

and i remember those special days when we'd go to the BIG library,

the one downtown, that which in my mind towered over the whole

of the city because it was where knowledge reigned and smiled

benevolently upon we, the little people...

i remember not just an aisle of my own, but an entire floor, full of color and tables and special chairs and cool little rooms and the computers on which i first learned to type and the sign that hung above the stairs that said i'd found myself just right, right there in the world where words lived...

i remember just how much i'd give to be able to go, how good i would try to be, how eager to be obedient so i'd get my chance to go the library...

i remember how happy i was in my world of words...

it's just not the same anymore...

the world is so fast now...

the words are so much more plentiful but so much more painful...

the words rush into our spaces, run into our faces, screaming and clamoring for our every second and attention...

the words don't wait in patience and silence, safe in their sanctums of serenity and reverence, but rather force themselves into our consciousness with neither thought nor regard...

the words are now wars that even our children are forced to fight...

and that isn't right...

it's not right that we no longer have those quiet and pretty spaces, those places where we can retreat into our silent, sacred havens...

the raven has squawked his 'nevermore'...

sure, they still exist; libraries still stand; the books still call...

but do we call back...

or maybe it's just that we've all stopped to pick up the phone...

Who was the person that touched you?

Who was the person that stole your innocence?

Who was the person that told you sex equaled silence and

secrets were attractive and that acting was how grown folks showed

they were in love?

Who was it that smelled of darkness,

Who felt like pain and looked like shame and sounded like evil

come alive?

Who forced your dreams to hide,

Down deep in a place locked against the light, down deep where

you held your will to fight, down deep where you knew that none

of this was right, down deep in that deep place.

Can you remember their face?

Can you ever forget.

Not yet.

Not now.

Not quite.

Not tonight or today or tomorrow or the next one either,

Not even should fire consume the sun and leave the world in

broken ashes,

Not even should the trumpet of redemption sound and we be

denied its calling,

Not even if that bastard begged with bloody tears and bruised lips and broken hands and the stench of perfume and in that room, in that cage, in that darkness that fuels this rage I scream "Not yet!"

Cause I can't forget.

Because I won't.

Because I shouldn't.

But I'll forgive.

I'll forgive so i can live.

Not for them; they can burn in the hottest hell that's unimaginable.

No, I forgive for me.

I forgive for my peace.

I forgive for my life, because my life is mine and I claim it.

Who was the person who touched you?

And who was it that set you free?

haikus

1.

Sunlight and silence

Cherry blossoms dance and fly

As the wind sings on

2.

If I could kiss you,

Were I to really taste you,

Would I get enough...

3.

She was like honey

And they call me Winnie Pooh.

Here's what this mouf do...

(ha)

4.

There's a quiet praise

Steady like heartbeats and hope

Honed by faith and fate

5.

I wrote her a smile

She read it against her lips

And so kissed my heart

haiku 2

words fill ev'ry space
life, itself, makes no mistakes
which path do dreams take?

i thought us a gift,
a present wrapped in laughter
a joy pure and blessed

but silence came still
and words once spoke are gone now
their echoes drifting

yet the dream remains,
yet those words fill ev'ry space
love 'twas no mistake...

haiku 3

He said, "Son, listen;
Ain't no sense in being mad.
You played and you lost.

Life's full of losing.
You think everything works out?
You think it's perfect?

Listen to me, son;
Let an old cat get you right:
You win some, lose most.

But you still play, boy.
That's the secret of winning.
You play and you fight.

Cause fighting is life.
Fighting is what makes you strong,
And the strong survive.

So listen to me.
Listen with your eyes and heart.
Listen and you'll learn."

He sat back and smiled,

Knowing it would take awhile,

But I'd understand.

That man's gone on now.

Time and God called his number.

He earned his reward.

But I'm still listening;

I'm still listening and learning.

Learning from his song...

I be's black.

I BE'S black.

I be's dark

I be's colored, I be's negro, I be's Afro-American ,

I be's chocolate, I be's midnight.

I be's black.

But I ain't nigger.

I ain't nigga.

I ain't nigguh or my nig.

I ain't boy, I ain't jungle bunny, I ain't spook, I ain't spade, I ain't spear chucker, I ain't porch monkey, I ain't coon, I ain't moon cricket.

I ain't statistic.

I ain't deadbeat.

I ain't dead.

I ain't fatherless home.

I ain't abandonment.

I ain't broken, though they've tried.

I ain't shamed of my black pride.

I'm black deep down to the inside.

I'm black and I thrive.

I am melanin and matrimony and metaphysics.

I am pyramid builder.

I am sun capturer.

I am scroll writer.

I am knowledge deliverer.

I am philosopher's philosopher, astronomer's astrolabe, navigator's lines of lay.

I am black every single which way.

I am the soul and solace, peace and purpose.

I am eternal.

I am supernal.

I am forever and existing.

I am the sound, the silence and the listening.

And I am shouting, Hear, now, this thing:

I be's black.

Black what I be.

And

I

Be

beautiful

i want to sit in silence and sing to the stars…

i want to listen to the moonlight as it tells tales of the past, present, and a million nights yet to come…

i want to listen to the babbles of brooks and chuckle with the stones over a sunlit joke…

i want to know just where smoke goes when it wends its way into the wind…

i want to know nature and creation, life and light and laughter and every sensation in between, to crush the grass to my skin like a lover been gone too long, to know the song trapped in snowflakes in the dead stillness of winter, to taste harmony and heaven in the first blushes of spring…

i want to know these things, know them better than my next breath, better than my last, better than forever and every fleeting past, i desire to know these things…

i want to sing a song to which words cannot exist…

i want to script spirituality and solace and brazenness and bliss…

i want to capture and cajole and caress all of this…

i want to know just how deep life can go…

and maybe, in turn, life will want to know of me…

you living so fast, baby girl; what you think you missing?

from kissing in pigtails to missing cycles and life fails, just rushing and rushing to a lost cause…

why you scared to pause, to be patient, to take a breath and pray?

what you think is getting away?

what you think you losing?

and you wonder why it's all so confusing…

"f*ck that nigga!"

"i hate that b*tch!"

anger and shame like a mid-spine itch…

they're killing you, love…

you think we can't see ourselves in the reflection of those tears you trying not to shed?

think we can't hear ourselves over the broken laughter you're forcing past bruised lips?

you think we can't smell the darkness on you, the endless lonely nights and the shouts of prayers cast against what you think is a careless heaven?

you think we've missed all that?

we haven't, love; we can't…

we just want you to recognize it, too…

life is hard, little one, and aint no shame in being broken on occasion…

aint none of us made it this far without a few scars marking our sins and our struggles...

aint no shame in being shamed when we picked the wrong lane and brought ourselves damage...

but shame you can manage; scars can be healed; pain, though real, aint nothing but a lesson 'bout a blessing if you're willing to open your mind and learn...

sometimes it's just your turn; sometimes you get to carry the L and while it seems like hell there's one thing i know to be unequivocally true: no matter how hard life gets, it's still livable, but the living's on you...

so live, lil mama, but don't just live: thrive...

it's a good thing to be alive...

it's worth it and there's a reason...

and even tho this might not be the best season, aint no flowers yet seen the sun 'less they first sat under the rain...

so do something special with that pain; ground it and grow...

you got no inkling of an idea just how far you got the gift to go...

but only if you slow down; only if you find your pace; only if you run your race and don't let the world run you over...

you're a four-leaf clover, lady, and the world is lucky to have you...

now go and be lucky for yourself...

She kept telling me that her head was bomb but all I heard was that her heart was blown to pieces, the shards piercing both her soul and good sense, hence my decision to avoid her altogether.

She was a purveyor of pleasure but was bound to her bitterness, frustrated, floundering, angry and hurt -- but, boy, could she squirt! The embodiment of lust but long since given up the ghost of love, she was a study in contradictions, afflicted by hope and apathy, happily throwing her body in spaces where simple conversation would do.

Yeah, it was crazy what that mouth do.

It told a constant lie of smiles and indifference and willingness to give everything she had, all bad decisions leading to empty beds and empty nights and empty promises and empty hands and a heart so empty it echoes the sound of her tears.

In the end she had traded sex for salvation yet wondered why she always felt like hell...

a poem is a story written from ink pressed from our soul, like olive oil squeezed from the ripest branches...we plant ourselves beneath our spirit and let poetry drip into our lives...

06/07/18

my tongue will script songs of starlight across the inside of your soul, melting melodies along the mainways of your mind, scribing sense and sensation in excruciating patience, forming patterns of life and living that even the midnight cannot replicate...

06/09/18

Poets speak the words
That others' soul's hold silent
Giving voice to hope

she cried across the page, each tear an ink-stained verse of curses and hopes and dreams deferred…rivulets of rage blotted the page and sang her song of sadness into the ether…and he heard her…sadly, he heard her…for he was a collector of broken things, shiny, broken things, and his collection was ever growing…he, too, though, was broken; broken and cracked and splintered around the edges…he'd hedged his own bets against hope and when that wager went wrong he doubled down, selling his soul to up the ante…happy only when hurting, he burst the bubbles of dreams like screams trapped in shiny iridescence…and you'd think he'd have learned a better lesson, having walked that woeful road so long and often…but he was a collector of broken things, of shiny and broken things, and nothing was more broken and shinier than she…every time she moved you could hear the crackle of her hope fraying in her soul…when she spoke, chips of her tomorrows fell from her lips and tinkled like glass against the ground…every smile was marred by the sharp points of her desire to be loved poking through the corners…so shiny, so surreal, so, so broken…and he was a hammer, fashioned of fury and loss and pain, every thud of his heart a sledge tripping into the concrete, bashing and crashing and crumbling his ability to do good…for he thought he was doing good, that this was actually an act of altruism…see, they thought that since broken pieces were the legacies of wholity, it was only right that their broken pieces were the path to build another…in their assessment, their brokenness was built to fit…so they clamored and crashed and clawed their way into each other, seeking in pain the path to salvation…and all the while, they were cutting each other to shreds, ribbons of well-wishes draping souls laid bare, tatters of time meant to heal having lost its appeal, love traded for lust and crushed by their rush to "fix" themselves in another's arms…how much harm do we do in our attempts to do good? and can good come from a place so observably bad? who knows…who can say…and, i guess, who cares, for they are still out there broken, still out there breaking, still out there dancing the dance of the hopeless, leaving the splinters of their tomorrows littered across the promise of better yesterdays…

A Blues for the Queen

I woke up early on a blue Monday, orange sun tickling along my eyelids, flashing red ribbons of promise.

Brown oak floors met walnut feet as street beats sung their way through my snug windowpanes, the city a serenade of life in full progression.

My smile danced along the back of this rhythm.

Today was gonna be a blessing, cause today she and me had a date.

Fate had found its destiny and the guarantee was greatness.

Let me describe this "she."

And as I begin, this I'm inclined to ponder: is perfect too firm a term?

In all seriousness, if this child was any prettier it'd have to be a sin.

Effortlessly she blended innocence and licentiousness like hues on a masters brush.

Lush lips curled into a soul-scrambling smile, skin fairer than the thickest cream dotted with freckles and familiarity, and all the while two eyes the color of warm rains in spring surveyed life and its myriad melodies.

Wisdom and wonder and wanton want were etched across her gaze and I appraised her like a gem beyond price.

So when she extended the invitation I didn't think twice.

She was fond of good food and better conversation, both filling soul and spirit in equal hearty helpings.

And I...well I'm both chef and savant, my words flavored with wisdom and wit, substance and salvation, spiced with insight, mellowed by maturity, plated to please the most palatial palate.

A mind fit for a queen.

For so I deemed her: royal and aloof, beautiful yet austere, close and equally distant like cupping the wind in your hand.

She wouldn't tolerate just any kind of man; this was abundantly clear.

Fortunately my bloodline is as rich as they come; prick me and I bleed purple with tints of gold.

I'm of old lineage, the age of dynastic empires and lyres lined with papyrus, of Horus and Isis and Set.

I'm as regal as they get and so our company was long foreordained.

This, I believe, my soul explained as I looked into her eyes, our spirits continuing a conversation we started before we were born.

And that makes sense; that's to be expected.

We've been connected since before there was time; this "now" is just the latest in an eternal series of meetings, repeating themselves over and again along the far-flung thoroughfares of eternity.

It's still sweet, tho.

Still exciting and engaging, and as we meet and eat our souls will play on repeat the endless rubato of our reunited existence.

This she.

This song.

This queen.

She, who is my blues...

fingerprints and nail scars trailed across her soul...stains of greasy desires, leering lechery, drooling and dripping damnation drowning the light of her innocence...lips curled in lust and denigration, hate and horniness, want and wanton disdain — these she bore on her back, her skin, her soul, her visions of the future, her memories, her dreams...screams weren't yet made that were loud enough to erase the echoes of tears...no amount of thrusting, grunting and groaning chased away the rusted remnants of a heart shattered by too many times hope refused to be realized...groans were "come back's!" on repeat, letters written and burned, whispers in the middle of the midnight into ears tuned to their own deceitfulness, touches gone rebuffed and regarded as waste and negligence...she, all of she, all of she given to give, left to live, dragged and drenched and drained and spent, drawn out and stretched and screwed and scraped and scoured by life...by life unrepentant...life unforgiving...life so cold and so, so unfair...life which she was left to live...

Where do you find yourself in a quiet moment?

Is it peace or turmoil,

Reflection or regret,

Silence or sadness?

Where do you find yourself in stillness, when you must be with you, when the echoes of distractions fade and the roar of solitary-ness is your sole companion.

What, then, do you find.

Who, then, do you find.

Where are you in that quiet, silent moment...

I am in love with the night sky.

There, in the darkness, I embrace the silence as the violence of stars burning cold and distant spins its song into the ether.

Arms wrapped around my knees like my heart wrapped around hope, sitting back on my heels as if grass heals all wounds, assuming that me and the midnight are twins and laughing at our inside jokes,

I am in love with the night sky.

Sometimes there's just too much sunlight, too much bright, too much rushing and rambling scrambling the song that was initially serenity.

The light has a way of ruining reverie, forcing the eyes into spaces that place way too much importance on nothing.

Everything and everyone exists to be seen, to be seen being seen, to preen and prance and lie and dance and wile their ways through a simulacrum of life.

And that's alright, I guess.

That's okay in its way.

That's just how that particular game plays.

But me, I prefer the moon.

I prefer the sparkle of the stars against my eyelids.

I prefer the deep and cloying caress that is that black against my skin.

I prefer to spend my life in the nighttime.

I'm something of an oddity that way.

But that's okay.

Cause I am in love with the night sky, and it has promised me that it will always love me back...

She said,

"I love you -- and that scares me. And because fear is close to pain and pain I've had too much of, if that's love, I'll pass."

Now, she didn't say those words exactly.

She said them with her actions, with calls not made and texts not returned and lessons about his heart that went unlearned, she wrote a book about brokenness and penciled his name on every page.

He wrote the sequel and titled it "Tears."

Cause he loved her, knowing that he shouldn't, knowing that it couldn't work, knowing that she would choose her hurt over the Heaven he offered.

He loved her.

Loved her right into his own heartbreak.

And yes, it was a mistake; yes it was ill conceived; yes they both felt relieved when it fell apart because they'd found their way back to the comfort of loneliness, but bless his heart, he still loved her.

He chose to love her, above and beyond what she was or did or had seen or experienced or lived through.

He loved her because she needed him to, to fix and find those broken places, to trace the scars of tears on faces that turned to pain much too quickly to stay next to happiness too long.

It was wrong; he knew that.

But it felt right.

He had the sight, could see beyond her today into what he prayed was her future, committed to be the salve to her soul and for brokenness a suture, swore that he'd love her despite her and do whatever that needed doing because that's just how love operates.

It was a mistake.

Yeah.

Definitely a mistake.

But a mistake he chose to make.

And were he being honest, one he's making still...

"Come back with your shield or on it."

An admonishment given to Spartan soldiers marching off to war.

Marching off to glory or death.

Often that glory *was* death, for they all returned that shield; they all came back; they all paid what was due.

This being true, I wonder if this is where we gained our obsession with scars, our reverence for relics of pain.

Once virgin skin raped by struggle and trial, soiled by sin and circumstance, beaten and riven and torn, the tale of trouble etched across our breathing canvas, a masterpiece monument to our willingness to bear pain.

A beautiful stain painted on this, our living, breathing canvas.

And so I wonder if this is from whence we learned our love of scars — and I wonder, too, if this is why we scar our souls with love.

See, we are broken creatures, marching into the fray, chained to our hope and dragged down with it into the muck of its betrayal.

We are beaten and bruised and battered by life, struck by strife, crushed in the crucible of smiles and laughter and late night calls and torrid texts and frail whispers in emails that fail to capture just where we lost the love.

For we have lost it.

Even those of us desperately clutching it, praising it, raising it like a banner o'er a field of disillusion and death, marching into a war we are typically too tired to win, trust the first casualty, lies the first shots over the bow, neither knowing or really seeking to know how, just charging into the breach through which our heart marched gladly.

Sadly.

Because we come back.

We eventually come back.

We inevitably come back.

Because this is the story not of our leaving but of our glorious return --

There, stretched out on our shields...

they say that you can't miss what you never had…i wonder if they could make tiny microphones and pass them into the wombs of mothers planning to abort…i wonder what those small lives would report…they have never had sunshine, never felt rain…they've never known hugs or heartache or homework or hunger or hope or homelessness…they've never had long talks or longer fights or sat up at midnight counting stars or tears…they've never had past due assignments or bills, chills from a good story or that crumbling feeling when you know you're gonna be the story that gets told…they've never had to look back and wonder just how much of their life was worth it — because someone chose to take that life away…someone chose the disdain of the disruption of their own day over a life that counted its existence in mere moments…someone who owned breath and breathing and life and its leaving chose to be the arbiter and end of both…so it may indeed be true that you can't miss what you never had — or it may be that ultimately we're blessed just to have the opportunity to have had it…

I think of thinking and then my thoughts become like clouds, fat
and fluffy clouds skipping along a high and errant breeze.

They dance across rainbows and run across riverbeds and sit on a
strand of sunbeam and waggle their toes at the world.

Curling up, over, and majestically, sailing an oxygen sea like proud
ships turned toward the main.

Or again in flips and dips, aerial acrobats stacking thousands of
memories high, plying outer space with their frivolity.

And sometimes it's just one little wee one, serious and serene,
gleaning greens and golds and blues and hues from the vaulted
vapors.

Stately and silly and heavy and, really, how many ways can't one
describe a cloud?

Or a thought.

Or the thinking.

So, yes, sometimes I think that my thoughts are clouds, high and
lofty and a little bit lonely, there up there in the rare world of air...

www.ingramcontent.com/pod-product-compliance
Lightning Source LLC
Chambersburg PA
CBHW051707090426
42736CB00013B/2579